Nature Credits: A Global Climate Solutions Fi...
Sustainable Finance, Biodiversity Markets, ESG Investing, C...
Adaptation, and Nature-Based Solutions

Copyright

Nature Credits: A Global Climate Solutions Finance Explainer on Sustainable Finance, Biodiversity Markets, ESG Investing, Climate Adaptation, and Nature-Based Solutions

ISBN (eBook): 978-1-991369-97-0

ISBN (Paperback): 978-1-991369-98-7

Published by Global Climate Solutions

First Edition, 2025

Cover design and interior layout by Global Climate Solutions

Table of Contents

Introduction

Nature credits are a new class of climate-related financial instruments designed to channel investment into the protection, restoration, and sustainable management of natural ecosystems. Unlike traditional carbon credits, which focus narrowly on the quantifiable reduction or removal of greenhouse gas emissions, nature credits aim to value and monetize a broader spectrum of ecosystem services—such as biodiversity enhancement, water regulation, soil health, and climate adaptation. These credits provide measurable, verifiable outcomes that represent positive environmental impacts, creating new opportunities for both public and private stakeholders to support nature-positive outcomes through financial markets.

The fundamental distinction between nature credits, carbon credits, and biodiversity offsets lies in both scope and intent. Carbon credits are tied exclusively to the mitigation of greenhouse gases, with projects assessed solely on their capacity to avoid, reduce, or sequester emissions. Biodiversity offsets, on the other hand, are typically used as compensatory mechanisms to address residual environmental harm from development projects, ensuring "no net loss" of biodiversity. Nature credits, in contrast, go beyond compensation and emissions mitigation by recognizing the interconnectedness of ecosystem functions and enabling direct investment in a wide range of nature-based solutions that support climate, biodiversity, and community resilience.

The emergence of nature credits is closely linked to the growing recognition within climate finance of the critical role healthy ecosystems play in building global resilience. By capturing the full value of ecosystem services, nature credits offer a mechanism to drive capital toward projects that not only deliver emissions reductions but also advance climate adaptation, foster biodiversity, and contribute to the long-term sustainability of both people and planet.

This Explainer is designed to provide sustainability professionals, institutional investors, donors, and policy decision-makers with a clear, concise, and comprehensive overview of nature credits as a climate finance instrument. The following sections will define their operational structure, explore their climate and strategic value, examine current challenges and innovations, and outline the pathways for scaling their impact within the broader global climate finance landscape.

Chapter 1: Mechanism Structure and Operational Logic

This chapter explains how nature credits function, detailing their foundational principles, issuance models, and market architecture. It introduces key stakeholders, credit types, legal frameworks, and operational processes that enable the creation, verification, and trading of nature credits within the broader landscape of sustainable finance and ecosystem management.

1.1 Conceptual Foundation of Nature Credits

Nature credits are innovative financial instruments that capture and monetize a wide range of ecosystem services, from biodiversity and water regulation to carbon storage and climate adaptation. Their conceptual foundation builds on lessons learned from carbon markets and biodiversity offset schemes, but advances the agenda by directly linking finance to broader nature-positive outcomes. Whereas early market-based approaches such as carbon credits or biodiversity offsets often targeted singular objectives, nature credits reflect the interconnectedness of ecosystems and the value of services they provide to societies and economies.

This approach arose as climate, biodiversity, and finance communities recognized that efforts to halt ecosystem loss or drive restoration required not only regulatory mandates or philanthropy, but scalable investment mechanisms. Science has clarified the foundational role of healthy ecosystems in ensuring long-term resilience—by sequestering carbon, providing fresh water, buffering climate extremes, supporting agriculture, and sustaining livelihoods. At the same time, growing interest in ESG-aligned investment and sustainable finance has driven demand for credible, transparent products that can deliver measurable impact across multiple environmental domains.

Today, nature credits are at the forefront of the evolving climate finance landscape, offering a practical, flexible way for investors, corporations, governments, and communities to support projects that generate quantifiable improvements in ecosystem services. They are increasingly recognized as a powerful complement to carbon credits, moving capital beyond emissions mitigation alone to support the full spectrum of planetary health and resilience.

1.2 Types of Nature Credits

Nature credits encompass several categories of tradable units, each reflecting the improvement or maintenance of specific ecosystem services.

Biodiversity credits are perhaps the most established type, representing measurable gains in species richness, habitat integrity, or ecosystem connectivity. These credits are generated by restoration of degraded habitats, protection of threatened ecosystems, or implementation of conservation measures that demonstrably increase biodiversity. The value and verification of biodiversity credits typically rely on established ecological metrics and baseline assessments.

Ecosystem service credits expand this approach by targeting specific services such as water quality, flood mitigation, soil fertility, or pollination. For example, rewetting a drained peatland can generate water regulation credits; planting native vegetation along rivers might generate credits for improved water quality and reduced soil erosion. The diversity of ecosystem service credits allows them to be tailored to local environmental priorities and market needs, from agricultural landscapes to urban settings.

Distinction from traditional carbon credits:

Carbon credits quantify only greenhouse gas reductions or removals, measured in tonnes of CO_2 equivalent. Nature credits, in contrast, recognize multiple benefits—carbon sequestration, but also

biodiversity, water, soil, and community outcomes—thereby
attracting broader investment and ensuring that projects deliver
genuinely holistic value. Many nature credit frameworks now
integrate or "bundle" carbon with other ecosystem services, offering
a more comprehensive value proposition than single-metric offsets.

1.3 Key Stakeholders and Roles

Nature credit markets are complex and multi-stakeholder, relying on
clear roles and robust collaboration for credibility and scale.

Project developers—including NGOs, government agencies,
private firms, and local organizations—identify opportunities, design
interventions, conduct baseline studies, and manage implementation.
Their expertise in ecology, land management, and community
engagement is vital for ensuring that projects deliver on
environmental and social objectives.

Landowners and local communities are often the custodians of the
land and must be engaged as partners. Successful projects depend on
respecting land tenure, ensuring informed consent, and providing
tangible benefits such as income, livelihoods, or shared governance.
Inclusive benefit-sharing models, especially with Indigenous peoples
and marginalized groups, are increasingly considered best practice
and essential for long-term sustainability.

Standards bodies and certifiers create the methodologies and
frameworks used to measure, report, and verify project outcomes.
Leading organizations—such as Verra, the Climate, Community &
Biodiversity Alliance (CCBA), and TNFD—establish protocols,
conduct audits, and certify credits, providing the market with
confidence in claims of impact.

Buyers include companies seeking to meet ESG or net-zero
commitments, institutional investors looking to diversify sustainable
assets, and public agencies or donors supporting national or global
nature targets. The motivations for buying credits range from

regulatory compliance and supply chain risk management to voluntary contributions for reputational value.

Market platforms and registries underpin transparency and integrity. Registries record issuance, ownership, and retirement of credits to prevent double-counting, while digital platforms enable transactions and market access. Technological advances—such as blockchain and remote sensing—are improving traceability, lowering costs, and scaling market participation.

1.4 Issuance Models and Pathways

Nature credits can be issued through several models, allowing flexibility and scalability across project types and geographies.

Project-based issuance is the foundation of most current markets. Projects identify specific interventions—such as reforestation, wetland restoration, or sustainable agriculture—then set baselines and quantify outcomes using established methodologies. After verification, credits are issued based on achieved results. This approach is highly customizable and enables innovation to match local ecological and community needs.

- *Restoration projects* focus on bringing degraded ecosystems back to health.
- *Conservation projects* protect existing habitats and biodiversity from loss or degradation.
- *Sustainable management* introduces nature-positive practices in working landscapes (e.g., regenerative farming, silvopasture).

Jurisdictional or landscape-level issuance aggregates multiple interventions across broader regions, such as watersheds, provinces, or ecozones. Here, government agencies or coalitions coordinate standards, monitoring, and benefit-sharing across diverse actors. Jurisdictional approaches are especially suited for scaling impact, aligning with public policy, and addressing drivers of ecosystem loss that operate at larger spatial or governance scales.

- *Government-led programs* can mobilize public and private capital for national targets or regional priorities.
- *Multi-stakeholder coalitions* align efforts, share risks, and pool resources for landscape-scale solutions.

Integration with financial mechanisms is expanding as green bonds, impact funds, and blended finance structures increasingly link investment returns to nature credit outcomes. For example, a green bond may finance a suite of restoration projects, each generating tradable credits as evidence of measurable impact. Blended finance uses concessional funding to leverage private capital, lowering risk and catalyzing investment in new or challenging contexts.

The adaptability of issuance pathways enables nature credit markets to respond to local realities, evolving science, and dynamic investor interest, all while maintaining rigorous environmental and social standards.

1.5 Nature Credit Lifecycle

Every nature credit follows a defined lifecycle that emphasizes rigor, transparency, and accountability.

Project origination begins with the identification and design of interventions, grounded in robust scientific and community input. Baseline assessments establish the starting point against which future outcomes will be measured.

Measurement, reporting, and verification (MRV) are the backbone of credit integrity. Data collection—using field surveys, satellite monitoring, or modeling—tracks progress against indicators such as biodiversity, water quality, or soil carbon. Transparent reporting and third-party verification ensure that outcomes are real, additional, and permanent, building trust for buyers and investors.

Certification and issuance occur once MRV confirms that outcomes meet standards. Accredited certifiers review documentation, confirm compliance, and authorize the creation of credits in a secure registry, giving each credit a unique identity and provenance.

Credit trading and retirement follow issuance. Credits may be sold on voluntary or compliance markets, through brokers or digital platforms, to companies, investors, or governments. Ownership changes are recorded in the registry. When credits are used to meet a specific target—such as offsetting a supply chain impact or contributing to net-zero goals—they are permanently retired to prevent double-counting.

This lifecycle is underpinned by ongoing monitoring, adaptive management, and regular stakeholder engagement, which support continuous improvement and safeguard environmental and social outcomes.

1.6 Legal, Regulatory, and Institutional Frameworks

The credibility and effectiveness of nature credit markets depend on robust legal, regulatory, and institutional support.

International guidelines such as those being developed by the Taskforce on Nature-related Financial Disclosures (TNFD), the International Union for Conservation of Nature (IUCN), and UNEP are critical for harmonizing definitions, methodologies, and reporting. These frameworks guide market participants in designing, verifying, and disclosing the risks and opportunities associated with nature investments.

Voluntary markets currently lead, enabling innovation and rapid scaling as companies and investors pursue climate and nature-positive goals. However, voluntary markets can face challenges of quality assurance, transparency, and consistency across geographies.

As markets mature, more rigorous standards and oversight are emerging to address these concerns.

Compliance markets are developing in response to growing policy mandates for biodiversity net gain, ecosystem restoration, and nature-related disclosures. Countries such as the UK and Australia are introducing regulatory frameworks that require or incentivize the purchase of certified nature credits for certain development or land use activities. The European Union's Sustainable Finance Disclosure Regulation (SFDR) and taxonomy for sustainable activities are also setting the stage for future integration of nature credits into regulated finance.

Evolving regulatory environments are increasingly harnessing digital technology—blockchain for registries, digital MRV, and real-time data reporting—to strengthen market integrity and efficiency. Effective institutional frameworks require coordination among regulators, market actors, and civil society to balance innovation with safeguards for people and planet.

As nature credit markets grow, continued evolution and harmonization of legal and regulatory frameworks will be essential to unlock investment at scale, ensure environmental and social integrity, and build broad-based confidence in nature as a foundational asset for global sustainability.

Chapter 2: Climate Impact and Strategic Value

This chapter explores the climate and biodiversity benefits of nature credits, analyzing their alignment with global environmental goals and the value they provide to investors and institutions. It examines the mechanisms through which nature credits deliver impact, as well as their integration within sustainable finance and ESG frameworks.

2.1 Linkages to Global Climate and Biodiversity Goals

Nature credits are directly aligned with the world's most important multilateral environmental agreements and frameworks. Their development and deployment help bridge the persistent gap between ambition and action, supporting governments and organizations as they pursue climate and biodiversity targets on the global stage.

The **Paris Agreement** under the United Nations Framework Convention on Climate Change (UNFCCC) calls for limiting global temperature rise to well below 2°C and pursuing efforts to limit it to 1.5°C above pre-industrial levels. Central to achieving this are both mitigation (reducing emissions) and adaptation (building resilience to climate impacts). Nature credits—by quantifying and monetizing investments in natural climate solutions—provide a vehicle to channel finance toward reforestation, wetland restoration, sustainable agriculture, and other activities that both sequester carbon and enhance adaptive capacity. Their versatility enables countries to implement, measure, and report progress toward their Nationally Determined Contributions (NDCs), the national plans at the heart of the Paris framework.

The **Kunming-Montreal Global Biodiversity Framework** (GBF), adopted under the Convention on Biological Diversity in 2022, sets out ambitious targets for halting and reversing biodiversity loss by 2030. Among its goals are protecting at least 30% of land and sea areas, restoring degraded ecosystems, and mobilizing significant resources for implementation. Nature credits, particularly biodiversity and ecosystem service credits, directly facilitate these ambitions by creating new revenue streams for conservation, incentivizing private sector participation, and enabling transparent measurement of progress. As financial mechanisms that drive funds toward biodiversity-positive outcomes, they help operationalize GBF targets and mainstream biodiversity into economic and financial decision-making.

Importantly, nature credits also create synergies with the **Sustainable Development Goals (SDGs)**, especially SDG 13 (Climate Action), SDG 14 (Life Below Water), and SDG 15 (Life on Land). By supporting integrated landscape management and resilience-building, nature credits empower countries to deliver on the interconnected SDG agenda.

Ultimately, the flexibility and accountability inherent in nature credits make them a practical tool for aligning national and institutional policies with the evolving priorities of global environmental governance.

2.2 Mechanisms for Climate Impact

The climate impact of nature credits is realized through both direct and indirect pathways that reduce greenhouse gas emissions, sequester carbon, and build ecosystem resilience to climate shocks. These mechanisms underpin the unique role of nature credits as tools for climate mitigation and adaptation.

Emissions avoidance and removals are achieved in several ways. Projects that prevent the destruction of forests, grasslands, peatlands, or mangroves help avoid the release of large amounts of stored carbon into the atmosphere—this is emissions avoidance. Restoration and reforestation projects, on the other hand, sequester carbon as trees and plants grow, actively removing CO_2 from the air and locking it in biomass and soils. The net impact of such interventions is quantifiable using established MRV protocols, ensuring that credits represent real, additional, and measurable reductions or removals of greenhouse gases.

Crucially, many nature credit projects also deliver **indirect climate benefits** that extend far beyond carbon. For example, restored wetlands moderate local temperatures, regulate water cycles, and buffer communities against droughts and floods. Coastal mangroves and marshes absorb wave energy and protect shorelines from storm surges—vital adaptation functions in the face of rising sea levels and extreme weather. Grassland restoration can improve soil health and water infiltration, supporting agricultural resilience and food security.

Nature-based solutions (NbS) are the engine of these climate benefits. NbS encompass a broad set of practices—restoration, conservation, sustainable land management, and agroecology—that leverage ecosystem processes to address societal challenges, including climate change. The effectiveness of NbS is now well documented: studies show that they could provide up to one-third of the cost-effective mitigation needed to meet global climate targets, while also delivering substantial co-benefits for biodiversity, livelihoods, and health.

Nature credits ensure that investments in NbS are quantifiable and financially attractive. By turning ecosystem outcomes into tradable units, nature credits enable the scaling up of projects that are essential for climate stability—projects that, until recently, struggled to attract adequate finance.

2.3 Biodiversity, Ecosystem Services, and Community Co-benefits

A core advantage of nature credits is their ability to generate holistic environmental and social benefits that extend well beyond carbon. By linking financial returns to a suite of ecosystem and community outcomes, nature credits drive investment into truly transformative projects.

Enhancing biodiversity is at the heart of many nature credit schemes. Credits tied to biodiversity restoration or habitat connectivity directly incentivize the conservation of threatened species, the rebuilding of ecological corridors, and the reversal of ecosystem fragmentation. These interventions support the survival and flourishing of plants, animals, and microorganisms critical to healthy and resilient ecosystems. As markets mature, the use of robust biodiversity metrics—such as species richness, population viability, or habitat quality—ensures that credits reflect meaningful, verifiable gains.

Beyond biodiversity, nature credits promote the protection and enhancement of **ecosystem services**—the benefits that nature provides to people. Projects that generate water credits, for example, improve the filtration and storage of freshwater resources, reduce downstream flood risk, and support sustainable agriculture. Soil credits are awarded for practices that enhance soil organic matter, reduce erosion, and increase fertility, all of which are vital for food production and landscape resilience. Pollination credits encourage the restoration of habitats for bees, butterflies, and other pollinators, underpinning the productivity of agricultural systems and ensuring food security.

Social inclusion and equity are also central. The most effective nature credit projects are those that meaningfully engage Indigenous peoples, local communities, and women. Participatory design, equitable benefit-sharing, and respect for traditional knowledge ensure that projects are grounded in local realities and create positive impacts for those who depend most on healthy ecosystems. In many regions, credits help channel new sources of finance into rural economies, supporting education, health, and long-term community resilience.

By bundling these diverse benefits, nature credits position themselves as unique instruments for integrated, sustainable development.

2.4 Strategic Value for Investors and Institutions

Nature credits offer compelling strategic value for a wide range of investors, asset managers, corporations, and public agencies seeking to align their portfolios and policies with long-term sustainability and resilience.

Portfolio diversification and risk mitigation are key advantages. Nature credits represent a new asset class, often uncorrelated with traditional financial markets and linked instead to tangible environmental outcomes. For institutional investors, adding nature credits to portfolios can lower overall risk, provide inflation protection (as land and natural assets tend to hold value over time), and create positive exposure to growing demand for climate and biodiversity solutions.

Reputation, compliance, and ESG reporting are additional drivers. As ESG standards become mainstream and sustainability reporting requirements tighten, corporations and financial institutions face increasing scrutiny regarding the environmental and social impacts of their operations and investments. Purchasing and retiring nature credits enables buyers to credibly demonstrate support for climate and nature goals, satisfy stakeholder expectations, and differentiate themselves in competitive markets. Many companies are now incorporating nature credits into net-zero strategies, supply chain risk management, and voluntary offset programs to deliver measurable progress and transparency.

Role in net-zero and nature-positive strategies is particularly prominent. Net-zero commitments—now adopted by thousands of companies and many governments—require rapid emissions reductions, but also the removal of residual emissions through credible means. Nature credits, especially those based on robust, science-backed NbS, provide a practical way to deliver these outcomes while contributing to ecosystem restoration and resilience. Beyond net-zero, "nature-positive" strategies call for proactive investment in the regeneration of nature and reversal of ecosystem decline. Nature credits supply the market infrastructure and transparency needed to track and verify progress toward these ambitious goals.

In sum, nature credits enable investors and institutions to align financial performance with planetary boundaries, future-proof their business models, and access new growth opportunities in a rapidly evolving global market for sustainable finance.

2.5 Nature Credits in the Broader Climate Finance Landscape

Nature credits occupy a distinctive, complementary position within the expanding architecture of climate and sustainable finance.

Complementarity with carbon markets and other instruments is central to their role. While carbon credits remain the primary vehicle for monetizing emissions reductions, nature credits address additional, often undervalued ecosystem services. Projects that generate both carbon and nature credits can "stack" benefits, creating integrated investment opportunities that deliver enhanced environmental returns. In practice, this means that restoration or conservation projects can attract capital from a wider pool of buyers—those seeking climate, biodiversity, water, or social outcomes—thereby accelerating market growth and project scale.

Leveraging private capital and philanthropic funding is another significant dynamic. Historically, conservation finance has relied heavily on public or philanthropic sources, which are insufficient to meet the scale of global needs. Nature credits create investable products that can attract mainstream private capital, drawing in institutional investors, impact funds, and corporates seeking to meet ESG targets. Philanthropic capital can be deployed in blended finance structures to de-risk investments and catalyze commercial participation, ensuring that projects with high social or environmental value but lower financial returns are not left behind.

Positioning within emerging taxonomies and reporting standards further enhances the strategic value of nature credits. As regulators develop new taxonomies—such as the EU Sustainable Finance Taxonomy—and global frameworks for nature-related risk disclosure (e.g., TNFD), nature credits provide tangible, auditable evidence of progress. This integration supports the credibility of green bonds, ESG-linked loans, and other sustainable finance products, ensuring that capital markets contribute meaningfully to global climate and biodiversity objectives.

By bridging finance, policy, and science, nature credits help build a resilient financial ecosystem that rewards stewardship of natural capital and incentivizes positive environmental action.

2.6 Monitoring, Impact Measurement, and Assurance

Credible monitoring, reporting, and verification (MRV) is the backbone of the nature credit system. Rigorous MRV ensures that claimed environmental and social impacts are real, additional, and permanent—building trust among investors, buyers, regulators, and communities.

MRV methodologies are continually evolving to improve accuracy, efficiency, and transparency. Leading standards bodies provide detailed protocols for baseline measurement, ongoing monitoring, and independent verification of outcomes. These methodologies encompass field surveys, biodiversity indices, water and soil sampling, and periodic reporting cycles. Third-party auditors provide external oversight, safeguarding the integrity of the credit system and mitigating the risk of greenwashing.

Technology plays an increasingly central role in MRV and assurance. Remote sensing via satellites and drones allows for high-frequency monitoring of vast landscapes, detecting changes in land cover, forest health, and water bodies. Blockchain technology is being deployed to record credit issuance, transfers, and retirements with immutable, tamper-proof records, increasing transparency and trust. Artificial intelligence (AI) is applied to analyze large datasets, identify trends, and predict risks, supporting adaptive management and continuous improvement.

As best practices mature and technology advances, MRV systems are becoming more cost-effective and scalable, enabling more projects to enter the market and more investors to participate confidently. This ongoing innovation ensures that nature credits deliver measurable, verified benefits and remain at the forefront of credible climate and biodiversity finance.

Chapter 3: Challenges, Market Barriers, and Innovation Outlook

This chapter identifies the practical, regulatory, and equity challenges facing the nature credit market. It addresses investor concerns, highlights emerging solutions, and outlines innovation pathways that can unlock market growth, strengthen integrity, and support the transition toward scalable, credible, and inclusive nature-based climate finance.

3.1 Practical Barriers to Scaling Nature Credits

Despite their promise, nature credit markets face several practical barriers that hinder large-scale adoption, liquidity, and impact. Among the most significant are fragmented demand and supply, the ongoing challenge of standardization and quality assurance, and the limited depth of active, mature markets.

Fragmented demand and supply is a fundamental challenge. The market for nature credits is still in its infancy, with a relatively small number of buyers and sellers compared to established financial instruments such as carbon credits or green bonds. On the demand side, corporates and investors have varying levels of awareness, motivation, and ability to purchase nature credits. Some are driven by regulatory requirements, others by ESG commitments or reputational goals, but many remain hesitant due to unclear incentives or a lack of understanding of how nature credits fit into existing sustainability or compliance frameworks. On the supply side, project developers face barriers in accessing finance, building the technical capacity required to meet rigorous certification standards, and aggregating projects to achieve economies of scale. Many high-potential projects in emerging markets or rural areas struggle to connect with buyers due to lack of market access or prohibitive transaction costs.

Standardization and quality assurance challenges are another major obstacle. Unlike the relatively mature carbon market, nature credits must quantify and verify a much broader set of ecosystem services—including biodiversity, water regulation, soil health, and social co-benefits. Methodologies for measuring these outcomes are still being refined and harmonized. The lack of universally accepted standards can lead to inconsistent definitions, measurement protocols, and crediting rules across projects and geographies. This complexity can reduce investor confidence, inflate transaction costs, and hinder market integration. Quality assurance is further complicated by the diversity of ecosystems, cultural contexts, and project scales involved, making "one size fits all" solutions impractical.

Limited liquidity and market depth also restrict the ability of nature credit markets to function efficiently. Trading platforms and registries are still evolving, and secondary markets are nascent or non-existent in most regions. This lack of liquidity can result in wide bid-ask spreads, price volatility, and difficulties for buyers and sellers to match their needs in real time. The absence of robust pricing signals impedes the flow of investment, while the small number of standardized, high-quality projects limits the pool of available credits. Unlocking deeper, more liquid markets will require not only more projects and buyers but also trusted intermediaries, stronger data infrastructure, and credible, widely adopted standards.

Collectively, these practical barriers highlight the need for ongoing investment in market infrastructure, capacity building, and global coordination to ensure that nature credits can achieve their full potential as a cornerstone of sustainable finance.

3.2 Investor Concerns and Perception Risks

To attract and retain investment at scale, nature credit markets must address several significant concerns around integrity, credibility, and risk. Investors—whether they are corporations, institutional funds, or public entities—require assurance that credits represent genuine, lasting, and verifiable environmental outcomes.

Additionality, permanence, and leakage risks are central to market integrity. "Additionality" refers to whether credited environmental benefits would have occurred in the absence of the financed intervention. Investors want to ensure their money drives new, not pre-existing, outcomes. Permanence is the risk that credited benefits—such as restored forests or improved water quality—are later reversed by natural disasters, human activity, or lack of maintenance. Leakage refers to the displacement of environmental harm, where an activity protected or improved in one area causes increased harm elsewhere. All three issues can undermine the climate and biodiversity impact of credits, erode market confidence, and result in reputational or financial losses for buyers.

Double counting and integrity of claims are also of high concern. As nature credits become more integrated into global finance and reporting frameworks, the risk that a single credit is claimed by multiple parties (either across supply chains, countries, or reporting mechanisms) increases. Without transparent, interoperable registries and robust auditing, double counting can erode trust, invite regulatory scrutiny, and create confusion in ESG disclosures. Investors need clear, auditable proof of ownership, retirement, and use of credits, particularly when integrating credits into compliance or voluntary disclosure regimes.

Reputational and greenwashing risks present further barriers. Companies or funds purchasing nature credits must be able to demonstrate not only the authenticity of credits but also that projects deliver tangible community and biodiversity benefits. Media and civil society are increasingly vigilant about "greenwashing"—the practice of making exaggerated or misleading claims about environmental performance. If credits are found to be of low quality, based on questionable methodologies, or fail to deliver promised co-benefits, buyers may face public backlash, regulatory investigation, and long-term damage to brand value.

Addressing these concerns requires high-quality, independent certification, ongoing monitoring, and proactive transparency from all market participants. Only by resolving these risks can nature credits become a mainstream, investable asset class that appeals to the world's largest pools of capital.

3.3 Regulatory and Policy Constraints

Regulatory and policy challenges continue to shape the trajectory and credibility of nature credit markets. Inconsistent legal and policy frameworks across jurisdictions can slow progress, increase compliance costs, and create uncertainty for all actors in the value chain.

Inconsistent regulatory frameworks are a major issue. While voluntary markets have led the way in developing standards and practices, the lack of harmonized international rules leads to confusion over definitions, eligibility, and reporting. Some countries have clear legal frameworks that recognize and support the issuance and trading of nature credits; others have not yet addressed them, or actively restrict such transactions. Differences in land tenure laws, property rights, and environmental regulations further complicate project development, particularly in regions where tenure is unclear or contested.

Alignment with national and international policy priorities is also a key constraint. Governments are increasingly seeking to mainstream biodiversity and ecosystem services into economic and climate policy. However, integrating nature credits into national climate strategies, NDCs, or biodiversity action plans requires cross-ministerial coordination, legal clarity, and policy alignment. Regulatory inertia, lack of political will, or competing policy objectives can create bottlenecks or block the flow of capital. Without clear, stable policy signals, investors may be reluctant to commit to long-term, large-scale projects, limiting the overall impact and reach of nature credits.

The solution lies in ongoing dialogue between regulators, market actors, and civil society, aiming to harmonize frameworks, clarify rules, and build a stable policy environment that enables sustainable investment.

3.4 Access, Equity, and Benefit-Sharing

Ensuring fair and equitable participation in the benefits of nature credit markets is essential for their legitimacy, scalability, and long-term success. This requires attention to access, inclusivity, and the distribution of environmental and economic gains.

Equitable distribution of benefits remains a persistent challenge. Projects often take place on lands stewarded by Indigenous peoples, local communities, or marginalized groups, yet these groups may lack the technical capacity, resources, or market access to participate fully. There is a risk that benefits accrue primarily to large landowners, international NGOs, or external investors, leaving local communities undercompensated or excluded. Transparent, inclusive benefit-sharing mechanisms are needed to ensure that those who protect and restore nature are fairly rewarded.

Inclusion of Indigenous peoples and local communities is increasingly recognized as both a moral and practical imperative. Their traditional knowledge, governance systems, and connection to the land are essential for effective ecosystem stewardship. Best practice emphasizes free, prior, and informed consent (FPIC), participatory project design, and the recognition of customary rights. Building local capacity, supporting leadership, and sharing revenues or decision-making power are vital steps toward equitable and sustainable outcomes.

Addressing social and gender dimensions is also necessary for impact and sustainability. Women often play a central role in natural resource management, yet are underrepresented in decision-making. Projects that actively promote gender equality, youth engagement, and inclusive governance are more likely to deliver lasting benefits, reduce conflict, and achieve broader development objectives.

In summary, embedding access, equity, and benefit-sharing in the core design and governance of nature credit markets is fundamental to building trust, attracting investment, and supporting global sustainability goals.

3.5 Innovations and Pathways for Market Growth

Continual innovation is driving the maturation and expansion of nature credit markets, opening new pathways for scaling impact, attracting investment, and improving transparency.

New MRV and certification technologies are transforming project monitoring and verification. Digital MRV systems—using satellites, drones, and remote sensors—enable high-frequency, cost-effective monitoring over large and inaccessible areas. Blockchain technology is being applied to credit registries, ensuring tamper-proof records, real-time tracking of credit ownership, and automated retirement. Artificial intelligence and machine learning analyze complex environmental datasets, improving accuracy in outcome measurement and risk prediction. These technologies reduce transaction costs, speed up certification, and improve the reliability of claims, making markets more attractive to mainstream investors.

Integrating nature credits with other climate finance tools is broadening market reach and resilience. Blended finance structures, which combine public, private, and philanthropic capital, help de-risk investments and mobilize larger funding pools for innovative projects. Nature-linked insurance products, which use credits as a basis for payouts or premium reductions, are emerging to support climate adaptation, disaster risk reduction, and agricultural resilience. Green bonds and sustainability-linked loans increasingly include nature credit performance indicators, connecting debt finance to verified ecosystem outcomes.

Evolving standards and international harmonization efforts are strengthening market credibility and facilitating cross-border participation. Initiatives such as the TNFD, the International Union for Conservation of Nature (IUCN), and UN-backed frameworks are working to establish global norms for measurement, reporting, and risk management. Efforts to align voluntary and compliance markets, clarify legal definitions, and facilitate mutual recognition of standards are essential for building larger, more integrated markets.

These innovations, collectively, promise to unlock new investment, enable more projects, and accelerate the flow of capital into nature-based solutions worldwide. They also help ensure that markets evolve in a way that is robust, transparent, and fit for purpose in a rapidly changing world.

3.6 Future Prospects and Recommendations

Looking ahead, the market for nature credits is expected to expand rapidly as awareness grows, standards mature, and global climate and biodiversity goals drive demand. Achieving scale will require concerted reforms—harmonizing standards, improving MRV, and strengthening policy and legal frameworks—alongside collaboration among governments, market actors, and communities.

Key recommendations include: investing in technology and data infrastructure; building local capacity and ensuring benefit-sharing; aligning national and international policy; and fostering partnerships across finance, science, and civil society. With these reforms, nature credits can fulfill their potential as transformative tools for sustainable finance, channeling capital into the protection and restoration of the world's natural capital for generations to come.

Conclusion

Nature credits are emerging as a pivotal instrument within the evolving landscape of global climate and sustainable finance. By monetizing a broad range of ecosystem services—encompassing carbon sequestration, biodiversity enhancement, water regulation, and community resilience—nature credits offer a practical, scalable mechanism for aligning capital flows with the world's most urgent environmental goals. Their integration with international frameworks such as the Paris Agreement and the Global Biodiversity Framework positions them as an essential tool for achieving national and global commitments.

Despite practical challenges—such as fragmented markets, evolving standards, and equity concerns—ongoing innovation, technology adoption, and international harmonization are steadily advancing the field. The strategic value of nature credits extends to investors, corporations, and governments seeking credible, high-impact solutions for net-zero and nature-positive strategies, portfolio diversification, and transparent ESG reporting.

Unlocking the full potential of nature credits will require sustained investment in robust measurement, inclusive governance, and policy support. By addressing these challenges collaboratively, stakeholders can ensure that nature credits deliver measurable, lasting benefits for both people and planet. As the market matures, nature credits stand poised to become a cornerstone of global efforts to restore natural capital, build climate resilience, and secure a sustainable future.

www.ingramcontent.com/pod-product-compliance
Lightning Source LLC
Chambersburg PA